What do you call hemorrhoids on an Eskimo?

(see page 13)

What's the definition of a Jewish nymphomaniac?

(see page 31)

Why don't blind people sky dive?

(see page 45)

What do you call three lesbians in bed together?

(see page 82)

What do you get when you cross an elephant with a prostitute?

(see page 98)

Know why there's no toilet paper at Colonel Sanders's restaurants?

(see page 124)

Also by Blanche Knott
Published by St. Martin's Press

TRULY TASTELESS JOKES IV

TRULY TASTELESS JOKES V

TRULY TASTELESS JOKES VI

TRULY TASTELESS JOKES VII

TRULY TASTELESS JOKES VIII

BLANCHE KNOTT'S BOOK OF TRULY TASTELESS
ETIQUETTE

THE WORST OF TRULY TASTELESS JOKES
(HARDCOVER)

THE TRULY TASTELESS JOKE-A-DATE BOOK

Blanche Knott's

Truly Tasteless Jokes IX

ST. MARTIN'S PRESS/NEW YORK

TRULY TASTELESS JOKES IX

Copyright © 1989 by Blanche Knott.

ISBN: 0-312-91588-8   Can. ISBN: 0-312-91589-6

Printed in the United States of America

First St. Martin's Press mass market edition/July 1989

10 9 8 7 6 5 4 3 2 1

for Gary Singer,
who has to laugh

CONTENTS

ETHNIC VARIEGATED

What do you call someone who's half Indian and half Chinese?
  Uglee.

.

What's an Italian virgin?
  A girl who can outrun her father.

.

What do you call a Mexican in an earthquake?
  A jumping bean.

What's this? (Pull out the skin on both sides of your neck.)

An Ethiopian with a grain of rice stuck in his throat.

Three men were hired to dig a six-foot ditch for the sanitation department. Soon the Italian laborer turned to his Polish buddy, who was slaving and sweating along next to him, and asked, "Say, how come we're down here doing all the work and he's up there telling us what to do?" And he gestured at the third hired hand, an Irishman, who was standing atop the pile of dirt.

"Got me," said the Pole. "Why don't you go ask him?" So the Italian climbed out of the ditch and posed the question.

"Let me illustrate why I'm up here and you're down there," suggested the Irishman, placing his hand against a tree. "Hit my hand as hard as you can with your shovel."

The Italian happily obeyed, but the Irishman pulled his hand away at the last moment. His hands aching and stinging from the force of the blow, the Italian was content to climb back down into the ditch.

"So how come we're down here and he's up there?" asked his buddy after a few minutes had passed in silence.

The Italian thought and thought, looking all around. Finally he moved his hand up in front of his face and said, "Hit my hand as hard as you can with your shovel."

What's a WASP's waterbed?
  Lake Placid.

And a JAP's waterbed?
  The Dead Sea.

·

What do you call a Filipino contortionist?
  A Manila folder.

·

How come they canceled the Mexico City Driver Ed program?
  The donkey died.

·

How can you spot the Jewish Ethiopian?
  He's the one with the Rolex around his waist.

·

What do you call a pitiful Puerto Rican?
  Despicable.

·

What do you get when you cross a WASP and a prostitute?
    The Mayflower Madam.

                    •

What do you call two Vietnamese in a Trans Am?
    The gooks of Hazard.

                    •

The Ficorellis had just moved to New York from Italy, and at a welcoming party hosted by friends, Mrs. Ficorelli was cornered by a Mrs. Goldfarb for what seemed like hours. "And for our tenth anniversary my darling Irv gave me a beautiful, full-length sable," boasted Mrs. Goldfarb.

"Thatsa very nice," commented Mrs. Ficorelli politely.

"And for our twentieth anniversary my husband gave me a three-carat cocktail ring," continued Mrs. Goldfarb.

"Thatsa nice," said Mrs. Ficorelli again.

Pausing for breath, Mrs. Goldfarb asked, "And what wonderful things has your Gino done for you?"

"Well, right after we got here, my husband he send me to a very expensive finishing school."

"Really?" Mrs. Goldfarb perked up at the hint of some good dirt. "And what did they teach you at the school?"

Mrs. Ficorelli looked her straight in the eye. "I useta say bullshit. Now I say, thatsa nice."

                    •

What do you call hemorrhoids on an Eskimo?
   Polaroids.

.

Goose a Mexican ghost and what do you get?
   A handful of sheet.

.

Three sailors, an Irishman, an Italian, and a black, were stranded in a life raft with the captain after their ship had been sunk in a typhoon. After going through the emergency rations, the captain gravely announced that there was only enough food for three people. "One of you will have to swim for it, I'm afraid," he said, averting his eyes from the sharks circling the raft, "but to make it fair and square, I'm going to ask each of you a question. If you answer correctly, you stay; if you blow it, out you go."

   The three sailors nodded their agreement, and the captain turned to the Irishman. "What was the boat that was sunk by an iceberg?"

   "The *Titanic*," answered the Irishman with a sigh of relief.

   "How many people were killed?" he asked the Italian.

   "Three thousand, four hundred and seventy," blurted the sailor, mopping the nervous sweat off his brow.

   "Correct," noted the captain, turning to the black sailor. "Name them."

.

Why don't black and Chinese people intermarry?

Because their children would be called "chiggers."

⋅

When Dino ran into Tony at the corner one night, he asked, "Yo, where you going?"

"I'ma going night school. You t'ink I wanna be stupid like you?"

"That so?" retorted Dino, thoroughly pissed off. "So whaddaya learn in school, anyway?"

"You know who Georgio Washing Machine is?" inquired Tony.

"No, who?"

"He was the first presidente. How about Abraham Linguine, you heard a him?"

"Nope," admitted Dino.

"Boy, are you stupid," sneered Tony. "He was the president who freed all the eggplants."

Embarrassed and furious, Dino retorted, "So, if you're so smart, whosa Luigi Gondrevorta?"

Tony scratched his head. "We haven't got to him yet," he admitted. "Who's he?"

Dino roared with laughter. "You pretty stupid yourself. He'sa the guy been screwin' your wife while you at night school!"

⋅

How many Italian mechanics does it take to give your car a lube job?

Only one, if you hit him right.

.

'Arry, a young Cockney lad, was working at home one day when he cut his thumb. It was bleeding rather badly so he decided to visit the village doctor. The doctor confirmed that yes, it was pretty bad, but not so bad that it needed stitches. "Anyhow, I've an emergency right now," the doctor told him, pulling on his coat, "and haven't time to tend to it anyway. But there's an old folk remedy for cuts I learned from my father, and that's to stick the afflicted part up a cow's bum."

'Arry was mulling over this bit of advice on his way home when he encountered 'Arriet. "'Ello, 'Arry, what're you doing?" she asked.

"Well," answered 'Arry, "I've cut my thumb, and the doctor advised me to stick it up a cow's bum, so I'm out looking for a cow."

"I don't know of any cows nearby," said 'Arriet. "Do you suppose my bum would do?"

"I dunno," admitted 'Arry, "but I don't see why not." And he led her off into a neighboring field, where 'Arriet obligingly pulled up her skirt and bent over.

"'Arry," she spoke up after a minute or two, "that's not my bum."

"It's all right, 'Arriet," consoled 'Arry. "That's not my thumb either."

.

The man was taken aback when he walked into a bar in South Dakota and was told, "Sorry, we don't serve Indians."

"But I'm not an Indian," the visitor protested.

"Prove it."

"How?"

•

After the birth of his ninth child, Luigi decided that he and Giovanna should start using some kind of birth control. He went out and bought some condoms, but found they had a tendency to burst at the crucial moment. Finally Luigi shopped around until he came across a brand that claimed to be extra-strength, put on two, and started making love to his wife.

Moments later Giovanna was on the phone to the paramedics. "Quick, come quick," she screamed. "Luigi's backfired and blown his balls off!"

•

What's the difference between a teacup and a peacup?

A teacup is what the English drink out of, and a peacup is what Mexicans drive.

•

Why do Mexicans drive low-riders?

So they can cruise and pick lettuce at the same time.

Hear about the Kentuckian who threw himself to the floor in a fit of rage?

He missed.

What do you get when you cross a Mexican and an Italian?

A guy who makes an offer you can't understand.

An Irishman, an Italian, and a Pole were sitting at a bar. Ordering a drink, the Irishman said, "I hate this place. I know a place on State Street where I can get every third drink free."

"That's nothing," spoke up the Italian. "I know a joint over on the west side where every other drink is free."

"Oh yeah?" chipped in the Pole. "Well, I know a place on the south side where every drink is free and at the end of the night you can get laid in the parking lot!"

"No kidding?" asked his companions. "That sounds great—where'd you hear about it?"

"From my wife," the Pole told them proudly.

Why does an Ole Miss graduate put his diploma on his dashboard?
So he can park in the handicapped spots.

．

How many Purdue engineering students does it take to change a light bulb?
One, and he gets three credit-hours for it.

．

How do you brainwash a Puerto Rican girl?
Step on her douche bag.

．

And how can you spot a Puerto Rican intellectual?
He's the one who can read without moving his lips.

．

What did the little WASP scream when his school was burning down?
"MY HOMEWORK!!!!"

．

What do you call someone who's half Jewish and half black?

A Hebro.

.

An Irishman got engaged to a lovely Lithuanian girl, and when they went in for their blood tests, it quickly became apparent to the doctor that the husband-to-be had no idea what sexual intercourse consisted of. Taking pity on the bride, Dr. Jones explained about the birds and the bees and the coconut trees, but the vague smile on the young man's face was unconvincing. The doctor's second attempt to explain the ritual of the wedding night left the Irishman smiling and nodding but clearly baffled. So the good doctor gave it one more try, to no avail.

Thoroughly frustrated, the doctor instructed the young woman to undress and to lie down upon the examination table. She obeyed happily enough, and Dr. Jones, a humanitarian through and through, proceeded to demonstrate for the Irishman. For forty minutes he demonstrated. Finally, sweaty and exhausted, he hauled himself up on his elbows, turned to the fiancé, and said, "Now do you understand what I've been trying to tell you?"

At last a glimmer of comprehension came into the Irishman's blue eyes. "I've got it now, Doc," he cried happily.

"Good, good," said the doctor in relief, getting down from the table and pulling up his pants. "Do you have any further questions?"

"Just one," admitted the young man.

"Yes?" asked the doctor testily.

"All I need to know, Dr. Jones, is how often do I have to bring her in?"

What's the difference between a blue-eyed Aggie and a brown-eyed Aggie?

The blue-eyed Aggie's a quart low.

•

You may recall that not too long ago the state of Kentucky enticed Toyota to build a plant near the city of George-town, after offering the company a very sweet deal. Well, one day Martha Layne Collins, the Governor of Kentucky, was scheduled to meet with both the Pope and the president of Toyota. Very upset, her secretary rushed into her office with the confession that she had scheduled both appointments for the same time and that both distinguished visitors were en route. "Which do you want to see first?" she asked the Governor.

"I'll see the Pope first," Collins answered. "I only have to kiss his *ring*."

POLISH

What's it say on the front of a Polish grocery store?
   "Food for Rent."

   .

A Polish man went on a game show and won his choice of two VCR cassettes, *The Happy Hooker Goes to Hollywood* and *Snow White and the Seven Dwarfs*.

   "Your choice, Mr. Krzyinski?" asked the emcee politely. A ripple of surprise went through the crowd when the contestant chose *Snow White*, but Krzyinski went off happily with the cassette under his arm.

   When he got home his phone was ringing, "Stan, Stan," reproached his best friend, "what for you pick a silly kids' movie like *Snow White*?"

"You should know, Jerzy," explained Stan, "that I am never liking to go fishing."

•

How did the Polish man beat the rap when he was arrested for indecent exposure?

Charges were dismissed for lack of evidence.

•

Fred wanted to start his own business, so he saved his money and opened up a sex boutique. After a week or so, his friend Morris dropped in and asked how things were going.

Fred conceded that things had been slow the first few days. "I sold a few bits of lingerie, a couple of French ticklers. But the last few days, dildoes have really been moving."

"No kidding?" asked Morris.

"Yeah," Fred went on. "I was even starting to run low when this old Polish lady insists on the red plaid model with the silver rim. So I sold her my thermos."

•

Heard about the new shoelaces in Poland?

Velcro.

•

What do you call a cute Polish baby?

Adopted.

•

There was once a Pole whose very favorite color was orange. One day he went to the market for Kool-Aid, only to discover that there was no orange flavor to be had. So he bought a packet of cherry flavor, brought it home, mixed up a glass, and peed in it.

•

What did the Pole do when his wife informed him she'd just given birth to triplets?

He went looking for the other two guys.

•

Did you hear about the Polish editor who couldn't read his paper?

It was all Greek to him.

•

How does a Pole rob a drive-in window at the bank?

He puts his gun in the little basket along with a note that says, "This is a stickup."

When the Poles invented the toilet, how did the British improve it two years later?

They put a hole in it.

•

How did Polish people get to America?

The first one swam across and the rest walked across on the debris.

•

How come the Pole returned his necktie?

It was too tight.

•

Two boys from the Polish countryside were taking their first trip to Warsaw on the train. A vendor came down the corridor selling bananas, which the boys had never seen before, so they each bought one. The first boy eagerly peeled it, and took a huge bite just as the train entered a tunnel. When the train emerged, he looked across at his friend, pointed at the banana, and cautioned, "I wouldn't eat that if I were you."

"And why not?" asked his companion.

"I took one bite and went blind for half a minute!"

What should you do if a Pole throws a hand grenade at you?

Pull the pin and throw it back.

Why do Polish names end in "ski"?

They don't know how to spell "toboggan."

LETTER FROM A POLISH MOTHER TO HER SON

Dear Stanislaw,

Since I remember you can't read too fast, I'm writing very slowly.

You won't know the house when you come home—we moved. It was a lot of trouble moving, especially the bed. The man wouldn't let us take it in the taxi, which wouldn't have been so bad if your father hadn't been in it at the time. About your father—he has a new job with 500 people under him. He's cutting the grass at the cemetery.

There's a washing machine at the new house but it isn't working too well. Last week I put four shirts in it, pulled the chain, and I haven't seen them since.

Yesterday your little brother came home from school crying. It seems that all his classmates have new suits. We can't afford a new suit, but we're going to buy him a new hat and let him stand by the window.

Mary had her baby this morning, but I haven't heard yet whether it's a boy or a girl, so I don't know whether you're an aunt or an uncle.

Uncle Mike was drowned last week in a vat of vodka at the distillery. Four of his workmates dived in to save him, but he fought them off bravely. We cremated his body, and it took three days to put the fire out.

Anna got a factory job in the city, and I'm sending her some clean underwear. She says she's been on the same shift since she got there.

Your father didn't get much to drink at Christmas. I put a pint of castor oil in his scotch and it kept him going till New Year's. He came with me when I went to the doctor on Thursday. The doctor put this little glass tube in my mouth and told me to keep it shut for five minutes. Your father offered to buy it from him.

It only rained twice last week, once for three days and once for four. On Monday it was so windy that one of our chickens laid the same egg four times.

Your loving Mother

P.S. I was going to enclose $25, but I already sealed the envelope.

•

Heard about the Pole who snorted Sweet'n Low?
  He thought it was Diet Coke.

•

How about the Polish Jazz musician?
  He was only in it for the money.

•

Why is it the Poles have no luck raising chickens?
  They plant the eggs too deep.

•

An ambulance arrived at the Polish hunting school to find the instructor writhing on the ground with a number of bullet wounds in his groin. "My God, what happened?" gasped the paramedic.

  "He got confused," explained the teacher through clenched jaws. "My instructions were for him to *cock* his *gun*."

•

Why did the Pole marry his dog?
  Because he had to.

•

When the country girl spent a week visiting her cousin from Warsaw, she was taken aback at how rough and tumble his city life was. "Why don't you come and spend a week on the farm with me and my family?" she suggested sweetly.

This sounded like a fine idea, so the next day the two cousins headed for the countryside. The next morning the boy was awakened by the noise of something splashing into a metal bucket. He got up to investigate, and was relieved to see that it was only his cousin, milking the cow. "Can I try?" he asked eagerly.

After a few tugs and squeezes, the city kid turned to his country cousin with an ecstatic smile on his face. "How long do I have to do this before it gets hard?" he asked happily.

•

Heard about the Pole who—

Lost his girlfriend because he forgot where he'd laid her?

Wouldn't go out with his wife because she was married?

Took his pregnant wife to the supermarket because he heard they had free delivery?

Called his girlfriend Tapioca because she could be made in a minute?

Thought Peter Pan was a washbasin in a whorehouse?

Applied for a job as a lifeguard in a car wash?

JEWISH

First Hooker: "I just finished giving a blow-job to a ninety-five-year-old man."
Second Hooker: "Oh, gross!"
First Hooker: "No, Weinstein."

.

One day a JAP goes home and tells her mother that she's been raped by a large black man.

"Well, hurry, go into the kitchen, cut up a lemon, and suck on it," her mother instructed.

"Will that keep me from getting pregnant?" the JAP asked.

"No," the mother snapped, "but it'll wipe that stupid grin off your face."

·

A customs agent stopped an old Jewish man who had just emigrated to Israel and asked him to open his two suitcases. And in the first one he found over a million dollars in one-dollar bills.

"Excuse me, sir," he asked the old gentleman, "where did you get all this money?"

"Vell, I'll tell you," the old man began. "For many years, I traveled all around America and I stopped at all of the public rest rooms in all the major cities; I vent to New York, then I vent to Chicago, then I vent to San Francisco. I vent into the stalls vhere the men vere spritzing and I said, 'Give me a dollar for Israel or I'll cut your testicles vit a knife.'"

"That's quite a story," the customs agent said. "What's in the second suitcase?"

"Vell, you should know," the old Jew said, shaking his head, "not everybody likes to give."

·

Milton came into his JAP wife's room one day. "If I were, say, disfigured, would you still love me?" he asked her.

"Darling, I'll always love you," she said calmly, filing her nails.

"How about if I became impotent, couldn't make love to you anymore?" he asked anxiously.

"Don't worry, darling, I'll always love you," she told him, buffing her nails.

"Well, how about if I lost my job as vice-president?"

Milton went on, "if I weren't pulling in six figures anymore. Would you still love me then?"

The JAP fondly took her husband's worried face between her hands. "Milton, I'll always love you," she reassured him, "but most of all, I'll really miss you."

•

What's the definition of a Jewish nymphomaniac?

One that'll have sex even when she's just had her hair done.

•

What do you get when you cross a gorilla with a JAP?

Nothing. There are some things even a gorilla won't do.

•

Two kosher butcher shops were located across the street from each other, and the owners hated each other. Times were lean and customers few, so whenever a customer went into one shop, the other butcher would go out onto the sidewalk and shout, "Him? To *him* you give your money? He's a cheat, a goniff, a liar! His thumb's on the scales! You buy from that schmendrick?" And so on, and so on, at the top of his lungs.

Well, the HOBBH (Holy One, Blessed Be He), as you might guess, became increasingly displeased with this set of affairs, so He sent an angel down to the butchers. "Look," said the angel, going into the shop on the left, "you're going to have to learn to be nice, so I'm going to teach you a lesson. I'm going to grant any wish you like— but your competitor will get twice as much as you do."

The butcher was horrified. "You mean that schlemiel, that schmuck, he benefits twice over?"

The angel nodded gravely.

The butcher thought it over morosely, then suddenly his face lit up. "O Angel," he requested, "strike me blind in one eye."

BLACKS

What do you call two blacks in a shoe box?
A pair of black loafers.

•

Edith, who was black, was admiring a white acquaintance's clear skin. The white woman admitted that her secret was washing it in milk, so the next day Edith ordered a bathtub full from the milkman.

"Pasteurized?" he asked.

"No, only up to my stomach," she answered. "I can splash it up onto my face."

•

Heard the black version?

    Little Miss Muffet sat on her tuffet
    Eating her curds and whey
    When along came a spider
    Who sat down beside her
    And said, "What you got in de bowl, bitch?"

·

How do you get twelve blacks in a Volkswagen?
    Toss a welfare check in the back seat.

·

A South African businessman flew to England for a business trip and was picked up in a limousine. He'd never ridden in a Mercedes before, and kept staring at the hood ornament. Finally he broke down and asked the chauffeur what it was for.

The driver, a savvy Londoner who could tell from the passenger's accent that he was South African, decided to have some fun. "In this country it's legal to run over any black people we come across along the road," he explained to his passenger. "That thing's a sight."

Spotting a black hitchhiker, the chauffeur announced, "Watch—here's how it works." He stepped on the gas and headed for the black, veering away at the last minute. But suddenly there was a loud BUMP, and when he looked back in the rearview mirror, to his horror he saw the black man lying on the roadway. "Oh, my God," he gasped.

"That thing isn't worth a damn," spoke up the businessman from the back seat. "If I hadn't opened the door, you'd have missed him."

•

What do you call a black girl with no brothers?
   A virgin.

•

Shirlene had her suitcase packed and set it down in front of her boyfriend with a thump. "Okay, Leroy, I'se ready to go to Florida."

"What you talking 'bout, girl?" asked Leroy. "I never said nothing 'bout takin' you to Florida."

"But Leroy," pouted Shirlene, "You tole me when I turned sixteen you was takin' me to Florida."

Leroy set down his paper and scratched his head in puzzlement. Then a smile broke out over his face. "Shirlene, honey," he explained, "I tole you I was gonna tampa with ya!"

•

Heard about the new college fraternity called Sigma Jig?
   You have to have two blackballs to get in.

•

Just before the wedding date was to be set, Titus sits Shonda down and declares, "Fo' Ah marries yo', Ah gots to have yo' vital statistics."

"Mah statistics?" she exclaims. "What 'bout yo' *one* vital statistic?"

"Dat's two inches, honeychile," says Titus with a smile.

"Two inches!"

"Das right. Two inches from the flo'."

.

Where do cocoons come from?

M-M-M-Mississippi.

.

What do you call a black man in Bangkok?

A Tycoon.

.

What do you call lipstick for blacks?

Mop 'N Glow.

.

What do you call three blacks at a Klan barbecue?

Charcoal.

How do you make a black person nervous?

Take him to an auction.

•

If you have ten black guys and one white guy together, what do you call the white?

The quarterback.

And if you have one thousand blacks and one white, what do you call the white?

Warden.

•

Did you hear about Evel Knievel's cousin, Ku Klux Knievel?

He tried to jump over seventeen blacks—with a steamroller.

•

Jackson was recruited off the street to be in a police lineup on a rape case. When the police brought in the victim, Jackson spoke right up. "Yep, that's her!"

•

The top brass at NASA was getting flak about never having sent a black man to the moon, so the next moon shot went up with a black astronaut aboard. The only hitch was that the decision had been so sudden that the fellow hadn't even been briefed. His only instructions were to strap himself in, wait till he reached an altitude of five miles, and remove his helmet. The craft was on complete automatic pilot, so Mission Control wasn't too worried.

On the way up the astronaut had plenty of time to reflect on his role as the token black, on what racist assholes ran NASA. If only he could prove it, could find some hard evidence. As he was musing, the spacecraft reached the designated altitude, and as the astronaut removed his helmet, he was startled to hear a noise from elsewhere on the ship. Investigating, he was shocked to come across another passenger, a chimpanzee in full astronaut garb! The monkey, too, had just removed his helmet, but it seemed to be studying a computer terminal in front of its seat.

I don't have a terminal, the astronaut thought to himself. What's going on here? Looking over the chimp's shoulders, he saw that the screen contained a list of operating instructions for the mission's data-gathering operations. His worst fears were confirmed when, in shock, he read the last item on the list:

1800 HOURS—FEED THE ASTRONAUT.

.

Why do the lions in Africa go around licking each other's rear ends?

To get the taste of native out of their mouths.

What's a hula hoop?
   A teething ring for black babies.

Did you hear that the KKK named Marvin Gaye the Father
of the Year?

HANDICAPPED

What do you call a guy with no arms and legs who cuts himself every time he shaves?
   Nick.

.

What happened when the leper's mom died?
   He fell apart.

.

What's a leper's favorite song?
   "Hands Across America."

What did Helen Keller say when someone handed her a cheese grater?
"That's the most violent story I've ever read."

·

What do you call a hippy with no legs?
A veteran.

·

Why don't midgets use Tampax?
They trip on the strings.

·

What do you call a one-legged ballerina's costume?
A one-one.

·

Seen the new medic-alert tags for epileptics?
They say, "I am not break dancing."

·

What do you call a fight between two test-tube babies?

Jar Wars!

Why do babies have soft spots on their heads?

So that if there's a fire in the hospital, the nurses can carry out five with each hand.

What's 34.5?

Sixty-nine for midgets.

"Yeah, Doc, what's the news?" answered Fred when his doctor called with his test results.

"I have some bad news and some really bad news," admitted the doctor. "The bad news is that you only have twenty-four hours to live."

"Oh my God," gasped Fred, sinking to his knees. "What could be worse news than that?"

"I couldn't get hold of you yesterday."

What's white and goes up?

A retarded snowflake.

What does a cannibal use to cook a person with epilepsy?
  Shake'N Bake.

•

Bumper Sticker seen in Ohio:
  ILLITERATE?
  WRITE FOR FREE HELP

•

If a waitress with one leg is called Eileen—
  and a Japanese waitress with one leg is called Irene—
  where do they work?
  At the I-Hop!

•

What do a blind gopher and a male virgin have in common?
  They're both praying they'll find the right hole.

•

The deaf-mute ran out of rubbers, so he walked into the drugstore, unzipped his fly, and laid his cock on the counter. Taking out a dollar, he put it down in front of the pharmacist and pointed expectantly at his penis.

The pharmacist looked him over, unzipped his own fly, and laid his own cock on the counter opposite the mute's. Verifying that his own was clearly larger, the pharmacist pocketed the dollar and walked away.

•

Why don't blind people sky dive?
  Because it scares the hell out of their seeing-eye dogs.

•

Heard about the new Cabbage Patch Doll with AIDS?
  It comes with its own death certificate.

•

What do you call someone who's psychoceramic?
  A crackpot.

•

And now for the definitive collection of No Arms & No Legs Riddles:

  What do you call a guy with no arms and no legs at a barbecue?—Frank

Waterskiing?—Skip

At your front door?—Matt

On your wall?—Art

But a good swimmer?—Bob

How about two guys who are good swimmers?—Swimming trunks

Lying in a hole?—Phil

Under a car?—Jack

In the bathroom?—John

In a bathroom in London?—Lou

In the mail?—Bill

On a stage?—Mike

In a forest?—Glen

In a spa?—Jim

Buried in the garden?—Pete

In a pot?—Stu

Who never loses a fight?—Victor

Stuffed in a box wrapped in cellophane?—Kit. Or Candy.

In the hospital?—Ward

Out in the rain?—Mac

In a lawyer's safe?—Will

Who's safe in a storm?—Lee

Who's still dangerous?—Cliff

Hiding in a liquor store?—André

Out in the driveway?—Ford

Swimming in the lake?—Doc

Being carried by a woman?—Percy

With no pelvis either?—Chester

Who plays five instruments at once?—Stump the Band

How about a woman with no arms and legs in court?—Sue

In a gorge?—Bridget

At a barbecue?—Patty

Who never leaves a sentence hanging?—Dot
In the garden?—Rose. Or Lily.
At the beach?—Sandy
In the orchard?—Cherry
Four women with no arms and legs on vacation eleven
months a year?—Jan, June, April, and May
Out in a field?—Brooke
With six legs, out in a field?—Bea
In a liquor store?—Sherry. And Ginny.
Visiting a Justice of the Peace?—Mary
Up early every morning?—Dawn
In a monastery?—Abby
Out in bad weather?—Gail
Who's euphorically happy anyway?—Joy
Out at Christmas?—Carol
Who never lets go?—Barb
Swimming in the harbor?—Kay
Who's a biochemist?—Gene
Who sits on a shelf?—Crystal
Who has no torso either?—Muffy

CELEBRITIES

Why couldn't Mozart find his teacher?
  He was Haydn.

·

Did you hear about the Polish Queen of Soul?
  Uretha Franklin.

·

What had eight legs and two breasts?
  The '84 election.

Why do Dolly Parton's boyfriends drink Busch beer?

Because they like to "head for the mountains."

One day Festus walked into the marshal's office and drawled, "Marshal Dillon, I've got this here swelling in my breeches and I don't know what to do about it."

"Well, Festus, what you have is called an erection," said the lawman reassuringly.

"But what do I do about it?" Festus wanted to know.

"The best way to get rid of an erection," advised the marshal, "is to go down to the stables, get a shovelful of horse manure, and rub it on your erect organ."

Just as Festus was in the process of reluctantly obeying Dillon's instructions, Miss Kitty happened into the barn. "What on earth are you doing?" she asked.

Blushing, he repeated the directions he'd been given.

"I have a better idea," said Miss Kitty coyly, lifting her skirts. "Why don't you stick it in here?"

Festus blurted, "The whole shovelful, Miss Kitty?"

What's stranger than Moby's Dick?

Lucille's Balls.

Why did Karen Silkwood die?
    Stevie Wonder was driving the other car.

.

What would you get if Ella Fitzgerald married Darth Vader?
    Ella Vader.

.

What does Mrs. Jolly Green Giant masturbate with?
    A mountain peak!

.

So what do the valley folk say when she's near climax?
    "She's a comin' round the mountain when she comes . . ."

.

Heard that Sylvester Stallone and porn star John Holmes were planning a movie together?
    It's going to be called "Ramrod."

.

Why haven't they cremated Colonel Sanders yet?
    They can't decide whether to do him regular or crispy.

·

Why are the Rams changing their name to the Tampons?
    Because they're only good for one period and have no second string.

·

What's in Miss Piggy's douche?
    Hogwash.

·

What's brown and lives in a belfry?
    The lunch bag of Notre Dame.

·

What did the seven dwarfs say when the prince awoke Snow White from her deep sleep?
    "Guess it's back to jerking off."

·

Entering his prison cell for the first time, Ivan Boesky was introduced to his cellmate, a six-four black serving twenty-five years for rape and manslaughter. "We gonna be in here for a long, long time," commented the cellmate.

With a nervous nod, Boesky acknowledged that this was so.

"Such a long time that it's kinda like a marriage, wouldn't ya say?"

"Sure," conceded Boesky.

"And in every marriage there's a husband and a wife, right?" the giant black continued relentlessly.

"Right," Boesky admitted, breaking into a cold sweat.

"So what yo' wanna be, de husband or de wife?"

"The husband," blurted Boesky with a sigh of relief.

"Fine," commented his roommate, settling his huge frame on the bottom bunk bed. "Now get ovah heah and suck yo' wife's dick."

•

Why was Madonna so lonely?
Sean was stuck in the Penn.

•

Did you hear about the time Dolly Parton was on *Let's Make a Deal*?
She won the booby prize.

•

What did Jessica Hahn say when she was caught in a whorehouse?

"I don't care what you say—I'll eat all the bananas I want."

.

Soon after his death, Len Bias found himself at the Pearly Gates. St. Peter spotted him and rushed over. "Come right in, we've been waiting for you," gushed the saint, and insisted on taking him on a guided tour of Heaven. "And don't feel too bad about your untimely death," he said, giving Bias a pat on the back. "We're starting a team up here, and we could use some talent."

Eventually they came to a very fancy gymnasium where some guys were playing basketball. Recognizing a few of them, Bias decided that Heaven might not be so bad after all—until he spotted an oddly dressed fellow running up and down the sidelines, screaming at everyone on the court. "Who's *that* guy," he asked, tugging on St. Peter's sleeve.

"Oh, that's God," explained the saint. "He thinks he's Bobby Knight."

.

What's the difference between Liberace and George Bush?

George's aides haven't killed *him* yet.

.

What happened when Tammy Bakker cried with joy to be back at Heritage USA?
  MUDSLIDE!!!

.

What did they find underneath all Tammy's makeup?
  Jimmy Hoffa.

.

PTL: Procreate, Then Lie!

.

What mistake did Gary Hart make in going out with Donna Rice?
  He should've let Ted Kennedy drive her home.

.

How many times does 50 go into 27?
  You'll have to ask Gary Hart.

.

What did Gary Hart say to Donna when the scandal broke?
   "I said lick my erection, not wreck my election!"

•

Young Beethoven's only interest was playing the piano, and one day it got on his mother's nerves. "You good-for-nothing," she screamed, "why don't you go out and get a job and help support the family."

"Aw, lay off, Ma," answered little Ludwig. "Someday I'll be a great composer."

His mother replied with a laugh, "Ha, ha, ha, HA." [Sung as the first four notes of Beethoven's Fifth Symphony.]

•

What did Rock Hudson get for Valentine's Day?
   Liberace.

•

Did you know IBM's now making a Reagan Commemorative Selectric typewriter?
   It has no memory and no colon!

•

Did you hear that the Chicago Bears are trying to recruit Dwight Gooden?

They want to put a coke machine next to the fridge.

MALE ANATOMY

One night this guy got so bombed that he went from the bar to the local tattoo parlor. And there the tattoo artist followed his instructions to have "I Love You" tattooed on his dick.

The next night he and his wife were making love when she suddenly went wild with rage. "What's the matter, honey?" he asked tenderly.

"I cook for you, I clean for you, I do everything for you," she screamed, "and now you're trying to put words in my mouth!"

.

The sergeant put his troops through a fancy drill, at the end of which they lined up three rows deep. Walking down the line, the sergeant stopped in front of each soldier, whacked him on the chest with his baton, and barked, "Did that hurt, soldier?"

"No, *sir*!" each replied.

"Why not?" yelled the sergeant.

"Because I'm in the U.S. Army, *sir*!" came the reply.

Continuing on, the sergeant saw a huge penis sticking out of the line and proceeded to whack it with his baton. "Did that hurt, soldier?" he boomed.

"No, *sir*," answered the private.

"And why not?"

"Because it belongs to the black guy behind me, *sir*!"

.

What's been the most effective means of birth control since the days of Adam and Eve?

Laughter.

.

What's the lightest thing in the world?

A penis. Even a thought can raise it.

.

The proud father gave his son twenty bucks on his sixteenth birthday and sent him off to the local whorehouse. His grandmother's house was on the way, and when she waved him inside to wish him happy birthday, he explained where he was off to. She insisted that he save the money and make love to her.

The boy returned home with a big smile on his face. "It was great, Dad, and I saved the twenty bucks," he reported.

"How's that?" asked his father.

"I did it with Grandma."

"What!" screamed his father. "You mean you screwed my mother?"

"Cool out, Dad, why not? You've been sleeping with mine."

•

If our ancestors came over on a boat, how did herpes get here?

On the captain's dinghy.

•

"Doc, you gotta help me," said Mr. Smith, walking into the physician's office. "I need a prescription for Sex-lax."

"Don't you mean Ex-lax?" asked the doctor.

"No, no, no," answered Smith testily. "I don't have trouble going, I have trouble coming."

•

How far could you see if you had a twelve-inch prick growing out of your forehead?

You couldn't see at all because the balls would be in your eyes.

•

Why aren't cowboys circumcised?

So they have some place to put their chewing tobacco while they're eating.

•

The big black man had been convicted of rape and sentenced to death, and finally the day came around. A murmur rippled through the audience when his pants leg was slit open at the knee for placement of an electrode, revealing the head of his penis.

"Don't laugh, gentlemen," he said. "If you was gonna be electrocuted, you'd be all small and shriveled up too."

•

What does the IRS have in common with rubbers?

Both stand for inflation, halt productivity, and cover up a bunch of pricks—and most people can see right through them.

•

A few days before his proctological exam, a one-eyed man accidentally swallowed his glass eye. At first he was worried, but when there seemed to be no ill effects, he forgot all about it.

Once in the doctor's office, the man followed instructions, undressed, and bent over. And the first thing the proctologist saw when he looked up the man's ass was the eye staring right at him. "You know," he said, coming around the table to confront his patient, "you've really got to learn to trust me."

·

Why do women have such big tits and tight pussys?
    Because men have such big mouths and little peckers.

·

What's worse than a piano out of tune?
    An organ that goes flat in the middle of the night.

·

One day a construction worker left the job a little early, and when he got home he found his wife in bed with another man. Purple with rage, he hauled the unfortunate offender down the stairs to the basement and proceeded to secure his dick in a vise. Utterly terrified, the man screamed, "Stop! *STOP!* You're not going to cut it off, are you? *ARE YOU?!?*"

"Nope," the construction worker answered with a gleam in his eye, "you are. *I'm* going to set the garage on fire."

.

Why do women have more trouble with hemorrhoids than men do?

Because God made man the perfect asshole.

.

Swallowing his pride, Fred finally made an appointment with the great foreign specialist and told him he wanted his penis enlarged. After examining him, the doctor prescribed a bottle of pills. "Each time you take one, say 'Wee,'" the doctor instructed him solemnly, "and your penis will actually grow."

Fred was barely out of the parking lot before he popped ten of the pills. Unfortunately he was so excited that he lost control of the car, and as it plunged over a cliff his squeal of terror—"Weeeeeeeeeeeeeeee"—was heard loud and clear.

Not long afterwards, a couple was driving down the same road. "Look, honey," observed the woman, "there's the hairiest telephone pole I've ever seen."

.

Heard anything about the "morning-after" pill for men?

It works by changing your blood type.

•

Garry was chuckling at the bar when his friend Steve joined him. "Women, they think they're so smart," he said with a sly smile, going on to explain that he'd eavesdropped on a phone conversation between his fiancée and her best friend. "She said, 'Garry doesn't know it yet, but the only time I'm putting out is when I want to get pregnant.'"

At this Garry doubled over with laughter, and Steve looked at his friend with some consternation. "I'd be pissed as hell—why aren't you?" he asked.

"Why get mad?" answered Garry. "She'll *never* know I've had a vasectomy."

•

What's the difference between a dick and a magic lantern?

If you rub a dick three times, the genie isn't going to be the one to come.

•

What's the definition of a tough competitor?

In a jack-off competition, he finishes first, third, and ninth.

•

Jack and Jill went up the hill to fetch a pail of water, but Jack fell down and got hurt. Early the next day Jack was complaining about the sharp pain in his groin, so Jill brought him to the emergency room for an examination. Only a few minutes into the doctor's examination, Jill left the room and ran all the way home.

"What happened?" asked Mom when Jill burst into the kitchen.

"Mom, Mom, Jack was masturbating!"

"Really?" asked Mom in a concerned tone.

"Yeah," said Jill. "The doctor took hold of his balls and said, 'Jack, cough.'"

•

There once was a bodybuilder who had to take a wicked piss, so he knocked a couple of people over on the way to the bathroom. When he finally got there, both urinals were occupied, so he tossed the nearest offender out the window. With a sigh of relief he quickly unzipped his fly, pulled out his eleven-inch cock, and began to urinate. Turning to the guy next to him with a smile, he said, "Whew, I just made it."

Frankly impressed, his neighbor said, "Wow—will you make me one too?"

•

What do you call a man who weeps while he's masturbating?

A tearjerker.

Jake and Jim were about to head out for another long winter trapping in the northernmost wilds of Saskatchewan. When they stopped for provisions at the last tiny town, the proprietor of the general store, knowing it was going to be a good many months without female companionship, offered them two boards featuring fur-lined holes.

"We won't be needing anything like that," Jake protested, and Jim shook his head righteously. But the storekeeper pressed the boards on them, pointing out that they could always be burned as firewood.

Seven months later, bearded and gaunt, Jake walked into the general store. After a little chitchat about the weather and the trapping, the storekeeper asked where his partner was.

"I shot the son of a bitch," snarled Jake. "Caught him dating my board."

FEMALE ANATOMY

Did you hear about the girl who was so fat she couldn't get out of bed?
  She kept rocking herself back to sleep.

.

How is a woman like a bank?
  She loses interest when you withdraw your assets.

.

The night watchman at a fancy funeral home was intrigued by the sight of a cork protruding from the vagina of a female corpse. Unable to resist temptation, he pulled out the cork, and nearly jumped out of his skin when "Moon River, wider than a mile ..." started playing. Quickly he popped the cork back in, stopping the music. Unable to believe his ears, he pulled the cork a second time and out came the familiar melody.

At that the incredulous watchman ran to the phone to call his boss. "You aren't going to believe this," he shouted into the receiver. "You gotta come over to the home right now." When the disgruntled undertaker arrived, the night watchman dragged him over to the corpse, pulled out the cork, and out came "Moon River, wider than a mile ..." as clear as a bell.

The undertaker grabbed the man by the shoulders and screamed, "You dragged me out of bed at three in the morning just to hear some cunt sing, 'Moon River'?"

.

What's another reason God created the orgasm?
    He couldn't wait for the second coming.

.

What's a nymphomaniac's nightmare?
    Meeting a guy with herpes and a huge prick.

.

One day Herb was in the mood for ice cream, so he walked to the nearby Baskin-Robbins and ordered a sundae. "And be sure to put a cherry on top," he instructed the waitress.

Fifteen minutes later the sundae arrived at his table. Pushing it away, Herb complained, "Where's the cherry? I'm not eating this."

Lifting her skirt, the waitress picked up the dish and sat on it. "Will this do?" she giggled.

"Well, okay," said Herb grudgingly, "but it better not have any stones in it or I'm not paying."

.

What's the best defense against rape?
    Beating off the attacker.

.

What are "Brownie points"?
    What you find in a future Girl Scout's bra.

.

The night before her wedding Maria pulled her mother aside for an intimate little chat. "Mom," she confided, "I want you to teach me how to make my new husband happy."

The bride's mother took a deep breath. "Well, my child," she began, "when two people love, honor, and respect each other, love can be a very beautiful thing..."

"I know how to fuck, Mom," interrupted the girl. "I want you to teach me how to make lasagna."

·

What's a clitoris?
A female hood ornament.

·

Hilary had tried every diet in the world but still weighed in at a hefty 320 pounds. Finally she gave up, so depressed that she decided to kill herself, and went out and bought a gun. The only problem was that she was unsure as to the exact location of her heart, so she called her doctor to ask.

"It's directly below your left breast," was the doctor's answer.

So Hilary hung up the phone and shot herself in the knee.

·

What's six inches long, has a bald head on it, and drives women crazy?
A $100 bill.

·

How do you make a hormone?
Don't pay her.

•

Who enjoys sex more, the man or the woman?
The woman.
How can I prove it? When your ear itches and you put your little finger in and wiggle it around and take it out again, what feels better, your finger or your ear?

•

What do you call a stewardess who gives a passenger a hand job?
A highjacker.

•

What's a lapdog?
An ugly woman who gives good head.

•

Three morticians were shooting the breeze at an undertaker's conference and the subject came around to what each considered his greatest achievement. Harry cleared his throat modestly and revealed that he had once had to deal with the remains of a man who stepped on a hand grenade. "It took me three days," he said proudly, "but it was an open-casket funeral."

"Not bad," conceded Jerry, "but listen to this: I got handed a construction worker who'd been run over by a steamroller, and he was ready for that open casket in two days."

"You guys got me beat," sighed Charlie. "My toughest case was a lady parachutist who landed right on the Empire State Building. It took me four days just to get the grin off her face."

.

How do Valley Girls part their hair?
    In the middle. (Spread your legs.)

.

Hear about the nympho who went to the beach?
    She was asked to leave the area after the lifeguard caught her going down for the third time.

.

Female: "Do you prefer panty hose or bare legs?"
Male: "I prefer something in between."

.

How do you pick out a paranoid woman?

  She's the one putting a condom on her vibrator.

·

What do spaghetti and women have in common?

  They both wiggle when you eat them.

·

Define virginity?

  A big issue over a little tissue.

·

Susie was desperate for her new husband to go down on her. After everything from subtle innuendos to outright begging had failed, one night she finally resorted to trickery. "Honey," she called breathily from the bedroom, "can you help me a sec? I've got a tampon stuck inside me. I'm sure you can get it out if you use your teeth."

  Disgusted, the husband pulled the diamond engagement ring off her finger and pushed it way up inside her.

  "Owww!" yelped the young bride. "What did you do *that* for?"

  "You really expect me to go poking around down there," snarled her husband, "for a lousy tampon?"

·

Why do women have two sets of lips?

So they can piss and moan at the same time.

•

What's white and black and red all over?

A half-breed on the rag.

•

During his many years in the Merchant Marine, Ernie had really been around, so when his ship stopped over in Singapore, he asked the madam of the local whorehouse for something exotic.

"I have just the thing," offered the madam, not in the least nonplussed. "Cyclops Susie."

Out from the beaded curtain behind the desk came a girl with one glass eye. As soon as she and Ernie were alone together, Susie popped out the eye, presented him with the socket, and urged him to go at it. Ernie swallowed nervously but obeyed, and when it was over, he was delirious with ecstasy. "That was the best I've ever had. Unbelievable! God, I can hardly wait till I'm back in Singapore," he gushed to the hooker.

"Don't worry, honey," said Susie graciously. "I'll keep an eye out for you."

•

What do you call pulling off a girl's panty hose?
  Foreplay.

.

Three women arrived simultaneously at the gates of
Heaven and were greeted by St. Peter. "There will be a
place for each of you once you have confessed your sins,"
he assured them, turning gravely to the first woman.

  "I married one man but I loved another," she admitted,
blushing, "so I divorced my husband and married the man I
loved."

  "Show her to the silver gates," St. Peter instructed a
minion, and turned to the second woman.

  "I loved one man, married him, and lived happily ever
after," went her story. St. Peter directed her to be shown
through the golden gates, and turned toward the third
woman.

  "I was a dancer in a cabaret," she confessed with a be-
coming blush, "and I pleased every man who came to see
me, pleased them well for the right price."

  "Show her to my room," said St. Peter.

.

A fellow met this girl and she seemed willing and he was
dying to try, so even though they didn't know quite what to
do, very soon they were doing it. "If I'd known you were a
virgin," the man said afterwards, "I'd have taken my
time."

"If I'd known you had time," she retorted, "I'd have taken off my panty hose."

·

Little Molly was taken to the beauty parlor for her first haircut. The strange surroundings intimidated her and she began to cry, but the hairdresser was used to children, and calmly offered her a cookie. Sure enough the little girl quieted down, so he began cutting her hair, but in only a few minutes Molly started up again.

"What's the matter, little girl?" asked the hairdresser solicitously. "Have you got hair on your cookie?"

"What are you, a pervert?" she snapped. "I'm only six!"

·

An amateur golfer playing in his first tournament was delighted when a beautiful girl came up to him after the round and suggested he come over to her place. The fellow was a bit embarrassed to explain that he really couldn't stay all night but that he'd be glad to come over for a while. Twenty minutes later they were in her bed making love. And when it was over, he got out of bed and started getting dressed.

"Hey," called the girl from beneath the covers, "where do you think you're going? Arnold Palmer wouldn't leave so early."

At that the golfer stripped off his clothes and jumped on top of her. Once they'd made love a second time, he got out of bed and put his pants back on.

"What're you up to?" she called. "Jack Nicklaus wouldn't think of leaving now."

So the golfer pulled off his pants and screwed her a third time, and afterwards he started getting dressed.

"C'mon, you can't leave yet," protested the girl. "Lee Trevino wouldn't call it a day."

"Lady, would you tell me one thing?" asked the golfer, looking at her very seriously. "What's par for this hole?"

HOMOSEXUAL

What job is extremely popular among homosexuals?
  Soda jerk.

.

How do you know that Rock Hudson didn't die of AIDS?
  He died of food poisoning: he ate a raw wienie.

.

A wino scraped together $5, bought and downed two bot-
tles of Thunderbird, and passed out behind a hedge in a
nearby park. Not long afterwards a fag strolled by and no-

ticed him. That's appealing, he thought to himself, and he rolled the wino over and fucked him. It was such a pleasant experience that he tucked $5 in the drunk's pocket and went on his way.

When the wino woke up he was amazed to find his pocket still had money in it. Hurrying over to the liquor store, he proceeded to spend it on wine and pass out in the same place, where the fag found him on his way out to lunch. Quite delighted, he had another go and tucked another $5 in his pocket.

This time the wino could hardly believe his good fortune. Again he got drunk and passed out, and again the fag found him and screwed him. Unable to believe *his* good fortune, the grateful fag tucked $20 in the wino's pocket and went home.

When the wino came to, he pulled the $20 out of his pocket. Clutching it tightly, he staggered to the liquor store and beckoned to the clerk. "Hey buddy, get me some good wine off the shelf," he instructed the clerk, "cause this cheap stuff's murder on my asshole."

•

What do you call three lesbians in bed together?

A ménage à twat.

•

What do Chinese homosexuals and black homosexuals have in common?

They both give bro jobs.

The English officer was not particularly pleased when he was assigned to a detachment of American soldiers in a NATO post, and his worst fears were confirmed when the American officer in charge came over and slapped him on the back. "Hey there, Nigel," he boomed, "call me Biff.

"You're going to like our camp," the American went on heartily. "We don't just sit around watching the grass grow and waiting for orders, you know. Take Monday nights. On Mondays we all get drunk as skunks."

"Count me out," said the Englishman stiffly. "I don't drink."

"Hey, pal, that's okay," the American reassured him. "You'll have some fun on Tuesday nights when we all get wrecked on weed."

"I wouldn't think of it."

"Not to worry," the American officer went on, "because you'll love Wednesdays. That's when we bring the local chicks over and the real fun begins."

"I hate to disappoint you, old chap," said Nigel, "but I do not consort with cheap women."

"You don't?" The American was clearly puzzled. "Say, you aren't one of those queers are you?"

"Certainly not!" retorted the Brit, highly insulted.

Biff whistled through his teeth. "Well, for sure you're not gonna like Thursday nights."

•

What do you call hemorrhoids on a fag?
    Speed bumps.

Hear the one about the queer who got kicked off the golf course?

He was playing with too many strokes.

.

Why do bisexuals consider themselves so fortunate?

Because they can get it at both ends.

.

What did one gay say to the other as they walked past the funeral home?

"Want to stop in and suck down a couple of cold ones?"

.

Over lunch in the hospital cafeteria, one doctor happened to mention to his colleague that he'd come across a nutritional breakthrough for his AIDS patients. "Pancakes," he explained cheerfully.

"Really?" commented his friend. "I wasn't aware that pancakes had any special nutritional value."

"They don't," the first doctor went on, "but they're so easy to slide under the door."

.

What was the gay snowman waiting for?
   The snowblower.

·

Why do bisexuals and gay men smoke cigars?
   Practice makes perfect!

·

What do gay kids get for Christmas?
   Erection sets.

·

What do you call a *Playboy* bunny who's a lesbian?
   Bitch.

·

Where do fags park?
   In the rear.

·

Hear about the gay guy who placed a condom on each ear?
   He didn't want to get hearing AIDS.

What was oral sex to Helen Keller?
A manicure.

·

How come there's so little fraternization on naval vessels?
Because the sailors seldom see each other face to face.

·

What's the difference between a priest and a homosexual?
The way they pronounce "A-men."

·

How did AIDS get into the country?
Up the Hudson.

·

What do you call a gay epileptic?
A vibrator.

·

One night in Greenwich Village a cop happened upon an armed robbery in progress. Giving chase, the cop finally fired at the robber and shot him dead. Instantly a crowd gathered around the body, and when a gay man happened on the scene, he couldn't see anything. "What happened?" he asked a bystander.

"This guy got killed by a dick," explained a spectator.

"Mmmm," mused the fag. "What a way to go."

RELIGIOUS

A man had been walking across a street, when all of a sudden he was clobbered by a hit-and-run driver and died. And he was welcomed into Heaven by St. Peter.

"Life here is very similar to life down there," the saint said, pointing down to earth. "You can still get hurt up here, but it's offset by the fact that nothing is illegal and everything is free. Just be careful, and enjoy yourself."

Amazed and somewhat bewildered, the man started out to take in the sights. Not watching where he was going, the man stepped off the curb and was almost run over by an Oldsmobile Cutlass. "Wow, who the heck was that?" the man wondered aloud.

"That was Mr. Olds," said St. Peter. "He's a driving maniac, but you've got to be careful if you're going to stay here."

The newcomer nodded and continued on. A minute

later, as he was carefully crossing over to a striptease joint, a speeding Cadillac nearly ran him over.

"God damn it! Who the hell was that asshole?" he screamed at St. Peter, who was still keeping an eye on him.

"None other than Mr. Ford. As you can see, the idiot enjoys driving fast," came St. Peter's reply. "I know it's tough, but do try to be careful."

The man made extra sure before he attempted a third crossing, but just as he was about to reach the other side successfully, a Maserati driven by some long-haired freak appeared out of nowhere and bumped him back across the street.

"Okay, who the fuck was *that*?" he screamed as he lay sprawled at the saint's feet.

"Keep your voice down," St. Peter hissed. "That's the boss's son."

•

A monsignor in his seventies, a middle-aged priest, and a newly ordained priest arrived in Penn Station en route to a religious convention in Pittsburgh. The young priest was given the errand of purchasing tickets, with additional instructions to obtain the change in nickels and dimes.

Young Father Patrick was taken aback by the ticket vendor's remarkable chest and shockingly low-cut blouse. Blushing furiously, he stammered, "I—I—I'd l-l-like . . . three pickets to Titsburgh, please." Then, realizing his error, he ran back to his colleagues in complete mortification.

"What's wrong, Patrick?" asked the middle-aged priest, Father Brendan, in concern, but Patrick was unable to do more than shake his bowed head and hand him the ticket money. So Father Brendan went off to buy the tickets. He, too, was taken aback by the voluptuous young lady behind the counter, who snapped her gum, leaned forward, and asked, "Can I keep you, Pops?"

Father Brendan gulped loudly and requested, "Three tickets to Pittsburgh, please?" Then, in a rush, he added, "And may I have the change in nipples and dimes?" Thoroughly frazzled, Father Brendan ran back to his companions, where elderly Monsignor O'Flaherty was unable to get anything coherent out of him. So the monsignor took on the errand himself.

Now despite his considerable worldly experience, even Monsignor O'Flaherty was rendered slightly breathless when the ticket-seller's endowments came into prominent view. "Can I help ya?" she asked.

"I would like three tickets to Pittsburgh," said the old priest calmly and slowly, ". . . and I would like the change in nickels and dimes." Collecting his change, he took a deep breath and added, "And when you get to Heaven, St. Finger's going to shake his Peter at you!"

·

Father Harris was motoring along a country lane in his parish on a spring afternoon when all of a sudden he got a flat tire. Exasperated, the priest stopped his car, got out, and assessed the damage. Luckily, a four-wheel-drive jeep rounded the bend and pulled to a stop behind the crippled vehicle. The door to the jeep opened and out stepped a powerful hulk of a man. "Good afternoon, Father," greeted the stranger. "Can I give you a hand?"

"Heaven be praised," rejoiced the priest. "As you can see, my son, I have a flat tire, and I must admit I've never changed one before."

"Don't worry about it, Father. I'll take care of it." And without skipping a beat, the bruiser picked up the front of the car with one hand and removed the lug nuts from the base of the flat tire with the other. "Why don't you get the spare from the trunk?" he asked.

"Why, ahh, yes, of course, my son," stuttered the amazed Father Harris. The priest rolled the spare around to the strongman, who casually lifted it up with his free hand, maneuvered it into place, and proceeded to tighten the lug nuts.

"Do you need the wrench?" the Father queried.

"That's okay," the fellow told him. "These nuts are as tight as a nun's cunt."

"Hmmm," mused Father Harris. "I'd better get the wrench."

.

The newsboy was sitting on the curb jerking off when a priest happened to walk by and chastised him. "It's a sin, you know," he told the young offender.

"Relax, Pop, I'm not a Catholic," said the newsboy breezily. "I'm a Christian Scientist and I'm screwing my girlfriend in San Francisco."

.

The Pope died and appeared at the Pearly Gates, where he knocked confidently and introduced himself to St. Peter. "I'm the Pope of Rome," he said. "Let me in."

"I don't know you," said St. Peter.

"Well, Christ knows me," said the Pope briskly. "May I come in now?"

"I'll check," offered St. Peter, picking up the phone. "Hey, J.C., there's a character out here calling himself the Pope of Rome and he says you know him." After a pause, St. Peter hung up and turned to the Pope. "He says he doesn't know you."

"So try the Holy Ghost," suggested the Pope.

"Say, Spook," said St. Peter over the phone, "there's a character here calling himself the Pope of Rome who says you know him." After a pause, St. Peter hung up, turned back to the Pope and shook his head.

"This is absurd," said the Pope testily. "Try the Father."

St. Peter obliged him. "Hey Dad, there's someone here calling himself the Pope of Rome and he says you know him."

"Yes, I know the son of a bitch," boomed God over the phone line. "He's the guy who's been spreading all those rumors about me and the Virgin Mary. Tell him to go to Hell."

•

What do you have when you sign up a hooker and two nuns for your football team?

One wide receiver and two tight ends.

•

Homer was speeding down the sidewalk in his wagon when it veered off and got stuck in the mud. This provoked him to cuss up such a storm that the town's priest came over and chastised him. "Homer, you know you shouldn't be cursing like that."

"Oh yeah," said the sullen little boy. "How come?"

"Because God's everywhere," said the Father gently. "Even, why even, on Billy Bob's back porch."

"Well fuck you, you goddamn liar," retorted Homer to the astounded clergyman. "Billy Bob ain't *got* a back porch."

.

What does the inscription INRI on the Cross stand for?
    I'm Nailed Right In.

.

Definition of an agnostic: a chickenshit atheist.

.

What's the worst thing about being an atheist?
    You have no one to talk to when you're getting a blow-job.

.

The priest leaned closer to hear the girl's confession. "So me and my cousin were alone in the house," she continued, "and we went up to my bedroom . . ."

"Go on, my child," said the priest gently.

"I lay down on the bed and Joe got on top of me and put his hand on my . . . on my . . ."

"Go on."

"On my pussy," stammered the girl, blushing behind the screen. "And touched me and touched me until I couldn't help myself."

"Yes, go on," directed the priest.

"I pulled down his pants and his cock popped out, stiff and tall," the girl went on, with a little whimper of shame, "and he began to shove it in me so hard . . ."

"Yes, yes, yes, go on," he urged, breathing hard.

"And then we heard the front door slam—"

"Oh, SHIT!"

CRUELTY TO ANIMALS

What do female hippos say during sex?
"Please can I be on top this time?"

.

How about female snails?
"Faster, faster!"

.

Hank was amazed at the length of the funeral procession going down Main Street. Watching for a while, he observed that the cortege consisted entirely of men and that it was led by a man holding a Doberman pinscher on a leash. When his curiosity got the better of him, he walked up to the man at the front of the line. "Excuse me for interrupting you in your time of grief," said Hank politely, "but I've never seen such a funeral procession. Would you mind telling me who it's for."

"It's for my mother-in-law," explained the mourner. Tightening the leash, he gestured down at the dog and said, "My Doberman here killed her."

"Gee, that's terrible," commiserated Hank. "But... hmmm... is there any way you might *lend* me your dog for a day or so?"

The bereaved son-in-law pointed his thumb over his shoulder and answered, "Get in line."

.

What do you get when you cross an elephant with a prostitute?

A three-quarter-ton pickup.

.

Jerry was showing his friend his bee collection when Herb pointed out that he'd better poke some holes in the top of the jar. "Otherwise they won't live through the night," he cautioned.

"Hell, what do I care," said Jerry wearily. "It's only a hobby."

. . . when feeling a [illegible] particles on [illegible]
When he [illegible] and the [illegible] of [illegible]
he [illegible] at the [illegible] of the [illegible] [illegible]
[illegible]

If what's green and red and travels a thousand miles an hour is . . . a frog in a blender;
And if what it makes when you add an egg . . . is frog nog;
What happens if you drink it?
You croak.

•

What do whales use for tampons?
Whitefish.

•

A man takes his two dead pet rabbits to the taxidermist and asks that they both be stuffed.

"No problem," the taxidermist reassures him. "And do you want them mounted?"

The man thought about this for a minute. "No," he decided, "just holding hands."

•

"Where did you get all these ugly bruises on your hips?" asked the doctor of the young woman.

"We were . . . uh . . . you know, having sex and . . ." the patient stuttered, blushing.

"Hmm, I see," said the doctor, as he gave the sore spots a closer inspection. "Please take my advice and switch positions for a couple of weeks until these bruises heal a bit."

"Oh, Doctor, must I?" pleaded the woman. "My horse's breath stinks!"

•

Two small birds have just perched on the windowsill of the girl's locker room when one turns to the other and says, "Will you look at the tushie on that bimbo!"

"Oh, I wouldn't know. I'm a titmouse myself."

•

Heard the one about the blind skunk who tried to rape a fart?

•

Three moles were tunneling away when the first mole remarked, "I smell carrots. How about you?"

"I smell turnips," said the second mole. "What do you smell?"

"Molasses," answered the third, and kept on digging.

•

Why do gorillas have such big nostrils?
    Just look at the size of their fingers.

·

What did the giraffe say when he walked into a bar?
    "The highballs are on me."

·

A young career woman taking her baby to the zoo for the first time made the mistake of passing too close to the gorilla cage. A hairy arm reached out and plucked the baby out of the stroller, and the huge mountain gorilla proceeded to eat the child before her very eyes.

A policeman arrived and spent over an hour trying to calm the hysterical woman, but nothing seemed to work. Finally he put an arm around her shoulders and reasoned, "Lady, don't take it so hard. You and your husband can always have another baby."

"Like hell!" she snapped. "You think I've got nothing better to do than fuck and feed gorillas?"

·

Why did the elephant stand on the marshmallow?
    So she wouldn't fall in the hot chocolate.

·

What do you call an adolescent rabbit?
  A pubic hare.

·

How about a guy who screws Bugs Bunny?
  Elmer Fuck.

·

Why did the chicken cross the road?
  Because Colonel Sanders was chasing it.
Why else?
  Because the Jewish mother wanted to make soup.

·

So why did the chicken go halfway across the line?
  She wanted to lay it on the line.

·

An American met an Australian fellow on the course of a business trip, and some time later he accepted his new friend's offer to come visit him in his little town "down under." One of the first topics of conversation that came to the visitor's attention was the big dance on Saturday night, which was especially confusing since he hadn't seen a single woman in the whole place. So he asked his pal how they could possibly be having a dance.

"It's true we haven't got many Sheilas in town, mate," admitted the Australian, "so about an hour before the dance, the fellas start lining up at the sheep pen to get a sheep to dance with."

"I can see settling for sheep," granted the American, "but why line up a whole hour early?"

"Cripes, mate, you wouldn't want to get stuck with an ugly one!"

.

My dog is sooo ugly...
   We shaved his tail and made him walk backwards!

.

Bumper sticker observed in Bloomington:
   FEED JANE FONDA TO THE WHALES

.

Once upon a time a nonconformist sparrow decided not to fly south for the winter. But soon the weather turned so cold that he reluctantly changed his mind and started south. When a storm came up and ice formed on his wings, he fell to earth in a barnyard, almost frozen, and when a cow crapped on him, the sparrow figured this was the end. But the manure warmed him and defrosted his wings, and, warm and happy, he started to sing. The sound aroused the interest of the barnyard cat, who cleared away the manure, found the chirping bird, and ate him.

The moral of the story:

1) Everyone who shits on you is not necessarily your enemy.

2) Everyone who gets you out of shit is not necessarily your friend.

3) And if you are warm and happy in a pile of shit, keep your mouth shut.

.

A suburban matron walked past a pet store and was unable to resist an adorable Pekinese puppy. Being in an erotic mood at the time, she named it Titswiggle, and she became devoted to her pet.

One morning just as she was drying off from her shower, she was horrified to spot her little dog squeezing through the fence and running off down the street. Panicked and stark naked, she ran downstairs and out into the street, but by then the only creature in sight was an early-morning jogger. "Excuse me, sir," she called out, "but I've lost my dog. Have you seen my Titswiggle?"

"No," panted the jogger, coming to a stop and pulling down his pants, "but do you wanna see my bird do the hustle?"

MISCELLANEOUS

When the first-grade teacher asked the new student her name, the little girl replied, "My name is Happy-butt."

"Impossible!" protested the teacher. "Tell me your name or I'm marching you right into the principal's office." The little girl calmly insisted her name was Happy-butt, and so she soon found herself standing in front of the principal's big walnut desk.

"Now, why don't you tell me your name, little girl," he suggested.

"My name is Happy-butt."

Having been warned by the teacher, the principal pulled out the new student's file. "Your name isn't Happy-butt," he corrected, reading her records. "It's Gladys."

"Glad-ass, Happy-butt—what's the difference?" said the little girl sadly.

Did you hear that Ford's reissuing its Pinto model?
    They'll be called "Chariots of Fire."

Mr. Wilson filed for divorce, and eventually it came time for him to plead his case in court.

"All right, sir," instructed the judge wearily, "please tell me why you're seeking a divorce."

"Because I live in a two-story house," answered Wilson.

"A two-story house! What kind of grounds for divorce is that?"

"Well," explained Wilson, "one story is, 'I've got a headache,' and the other story is, 'It's the wrong time of the month.'"

What's the difference between a nephrologist and a neurologist?
    The "p."

A man from the city decided to buy himself a pig, so he took a drive in the country until he came across a sign reading, "Pigs for Sale." Turning into the drive, he parked next to an old farmer standing by a pen full of pigs and explained his mission. Agreeing to a price of a dollar a pound, he picked out his pig, whereupon the old man picked up the pig by the tail with his teeth. "Ayuh," he pronounced, setting the squealing animal down, "that there pig weighs sixty-nine pounds."

Noting his customer's astonishment, the farmer explained that the ability to weigh pigs in this manner was a family trait passed down through the generations. Skeptical, and not wanting to be taken for a city slicker, the man insisted on a second opinion. So the old farmer called his son over from the barn, and the boy in the same fashion pronounced the pig's weight to be sixty-nine pounds.

Convinced, the man pulled out his wallet, but the farmer asked him to go up to the farmhouse and pay his wife, who would give him a receipt. The man was gone for a long time, and when he finally returned to the pigpen, it was without a receipt. "What's the problem, son?" asked the old man.

"I went up there just like you said," recounted the man from the city, "but your wife was too busy to give me a receipt."

"Too busy doing what?" wondered the farmer.

"Well, sir, I'm not exactly sure," stammered the man, "but I think she's weighing the milkman."

·

If a person from Mexico is a Mexican, and a native of San Francisco's a San Franciscan...

...is a person from Tampa a Tampon?

...is a person from Maine a Maniac?

A young woman was sitting on the bus cooing to her baby when a drunk staggered aboard and down the aisle. Stopping in front of her, he looked down and pronounced, "Lady, that is the ugliest baby I have ever seen."

The woman burst into tears and there was such an outcry of sympathy among the other passengers that they kicked the drunk off. But the woman kept on sobbing and wailing so loudly that finally the driver pulled the bus over to the side of the road. "Look, I don't know what that bum said to you," the driver told his inconsolable passenger, "but to help calm you down I'm going to get you a cup of tea." And off he went, coming back shortly with a cup of tea from the corner deli.

"Now calm down, lady," soothed the driver, "everything's going to be okay. See, I brought you a cup of nice, hot tea, and I even got a banana for your pet monkey."

•

The new bride was delighted when her husband offered to take the wash to the laundromat, but less than pleased when she pulled a mangled pair of pink silk panties out of the bag. "Jimmy, I told you those need to be hand washed in cold water," she scolded him.

"They're mine and I'll do as I damn well please with them!" he snapped.

•

After the construction worker had climbed twenty stories to the job site, he asked the foreman if he could go back down to take a leak. Not wanting to lose the time, the foreman balanced one I-beam across another, stood on one end, and told the worker to walk out on the other end to pee. But while the worker was relieving himself, the phone rang. Unthinking, the foreman jumped off to answer it, and the construction worker plunged twenty stories to his death.

The next week a team of safety inspectors came by to conduct a routine investigation, and questioned the ground crew about the accident.

"I think it was sex-related," offered one of the crew.

"Oh yeah? How do you figure that?" asked an investigator.

"Well, what made you look up was this guy coming down, his dick in his hand, and screaming, 'Where did that cocksucker go?'"

•

The nearest customer was five stools away, but that didn't keep Josh from leaning over toward the bartender and commenting, "Jeez, there's a lousy smell in here." A few minutes later he added, "It smells just like . . . shit." Puzzled by the origin of the stench, he moved closer to the other customer, and sure enough the smell worsened. "Phew, you really stink," he pointed out.

"I know," said the man apologetically. "It's because of my job." Seeing that Josh was interested in a further explanation, he went on, "I'm with an elephant act, and before each show I have to give the elephant an enema so he doesn't take a dump during the performance. Frankly, it's a tricky business, because I have to administer it quickly and then jump back. And sometimes I just don't move fast enough."

"Jesus," commiserated Josh, shaking his head. "How much do they pay you for this lousy job?"

"Eighty-five bucks a week," said the man cheerfully.

"You've got to be kidding. Why don't you quit?"

"What?" retorted the man. "And get out of show business?"

.

What do you get when a victim of Agent Orange marries someone with Acquired Immune Deficiency Syndrome?

Orange-AIDS.

.

Three women died and went up to the Pearly Gates, where they were instructed by St. Peter to take off their shirts for religious purposes. "Now why is it that you have an H on your chest?" he asked the first woman.

Blushing a bit, she explained, "Because whenever my husband made love to me, he wore his Hamilton sweatshirt."

"And why is there a big A on your chest?" St. Peter asked the next woman.

"My husband always wore his Allegheny sweatshirt when he was feeling amorous," she explained coyly.

"And you? Let me guess," said the saint, turning to the third woman and noting the M on her chest. "Every time your husband made love to you, he wore his Michigan sweatshirt, right?"

"No, smartass," she snapped. "He went to Wisconsin."

•

Define "egghead":
What Mrs. Dumpty gives to Humpty.

•

"Abe, go down and check. Please." It was two in the morning and still Rachel hadn't come upstairs. "Abe, see what she and that boy are up to," nagged Sylvia again.

Finally dragging himself from bed with a groan, Abe pulled on his bathrobe. At the foot of the stairs he almost ran right into the young man in question. Clearly on his way out, the young man collected himself and shook hands, saying, "Good night, sir."

Back upstairs Sylvia rolled over to see Abe smelling his fingers and grinning. "So what is it?" she demanded.

"Soon," answered Abe, "soon I think we're going to have a son-in-law!"

•

What's the noisiest thing in the world?
Two skeletons screwing on a tin roof.

A young man was walking down a long country road when it started to get dark, so he knocked on the door of the nearest farmhouse and asked whether he could spend the night. "Sure," said the farmer, "you can stay in the barn. Just don't put your dick in any of the knotholes in the side wall."

Thanking him profusely for his hospitality, the young man headed for the barn and tried to get to sleep. But eventually he was overcome by curiosity, and stuck his dick in the first hole. "Ahhhhh," he moaned in pleasure, keeping it in for a while. Then, even more curious, he moved to the second hole. The sensation there was so delightful that an "ooooh" of ecstasy escaped his lips. Finally he pulled out his dick and inserted it into the third hole. "Yeeeaaagghhh!" he screamed.

"Say, what was behind those knotholes anyway?" asked the young man casually the next morning.

Smiling, the farmer answered, "Well, the first one was my wife, the second one was my daughter, and the third one was me and my trusty pliers."

•

Taken the CRUEL AND UNUSUAL test yet?

Have you had any prior experience setting orphans on fire?

When your puppy goes off in another room, is it because of an explosive charge?

Can you agree with this statement:

> Guns Don't Kill People—I Kill People.

Do you understand the difference between a baby seal and a pelt?

Would you consider Bambi and Thumper fair game?

•

The man couldn't find his way around the unfamiliar drugstore, so he went up to the girl at the counter and said, "I'd like some Head and Shoulders."

She gave him a puzzled glance. "What's shoulders?"

•

Hear about the neurotic who attended his first orgy?

Now he doesn't know who to thank.

•

How can you tell if you have acne?

If a blind man can read your face.

•

A fellow was having a few beers at his local pub on a Saturday afternoon when he was approached by a man dressed all in green. "Know what?" the man in green asked confidingly. "I'm a leprechaun, and I'm feeling extremely generous. So generous, in fact, that I'm willing to grant you any three wishes you'd like."

"No kidding! Gee, that's great," blurted the lucky fellow. "I could sure use some extra cash."

"No problem," said the leprechaun with a gracious wave. "The trunk of your car is now crammed with hundred-dollar bills. What's next?"

"Well, I wouldn't mind moving to a nicer house."

"Consider it done," announced the leprechaun grandly. "Four bedrooms, three-and-a-half baths, up on Society Hill. And your third wish?"

"Well, uh, how about a gorgeous blonde?" suggested the fellow, blushing a bit.

"She's in your new house, waiting for you in a flimsy negligee."

"This is really great," said the lucky guy, getting down from his stool and starting for the door. "I wish there were some way to thank you."

"Oh, but there is," spoke up the man in green. "I'd like a blow job."

"A blow job?" The man wasn't sure he'd heard right.

"Yup. And after all I've given you, it doesn't seem like much to ask, now does it?"

The lucky fellow had to admit this was true, so in a dark corner of the bar he obliged his benefactor. As he pulled on his jacket and turned away, the man in green stopped him. "Just one question," he asked. "How old are you?"

"Thirty-four."

"And you still believe in leprechauns?"

•

What's red and blue with a long string?

A smurfette with her period.

"Hello there," said the vacuum cleaner salesman to the little girl who answered the door. "Would you like to buy a vacuum cleaner? Watch this!" Pushing his way into the house, the salesman proceeded to dump a pile of lint and coffee grounds out onto the shag carpet. "If this vacuum doesn't clean this mess right up," he boasted with a big smile, "why, I'll eat it right up."

At this, the little girl turned and left the room. "Where're you going, kid?" called the salesman. "To find your mom?"

"Nope," answered the little girl from the doorway. "I'm getting a plate and a spoon, 'cause we don't have any electricity."

.

There's a rumor that New York State's putting a roof over the Attica penitentiary exercise yard.

They're going to call it the Condome.

.

(This is a CB radio joke—keep that in mind.)
What do you call a robot's pubic hair?
Tin fur!

.

115

Two young hillbillies in love were necking on the porch swing. "Say something soft and mushy, honey," begged Nettie.

"Shee-it," offered Hiram.

•

Hear about the man who confused Vaseline with putty?
    All his windows fell out.

•

What branch of the service has seven openings for shuttle pilots?
    The Marine Corpse.

•

What does NASA stand for?
    The National Astronaut Scattering Administration.

•

As Judge Hawkins's retirement neared, he got feistier and feistier, and one day he let a drunk really have it. The defendant's license had been revoked years earlier, but he was still regularly hauled in on DWI charges. "Just why is it," boomed the judge from the bench, "that in the last twelve years you have appeared in my courtroom so many times?"

"Hell, Judge," offered the drunk with a sloppy grin, "it's not my fault if you can't get promoted."

•

Know what a hobosexual is?
A bum fuck.

•

Some "Crash of '87" jokes:

What's the difference between a pigeon and a yuppie?
A pigeon can still make a deposit on a BMW.

How about the difference between a yuppie and a bagman?
One phone call.

Did you hear they're staging a benefit for those poor brokers?
It's going to be called Stock-Aid.

What's "yuppie" stand for?
Young, Unemployed Professional.

•

Harry was watching his mother make dessert when she suddenly slammed down the spoon and ran to her bedroom with a measuring cup in hand. In just a little while she returned to the kitchen and carried on with the recipe. Soon afterwards in came Harry's dad, sweating and tucking in his shirttails.

"What's going on, Ma?" asked the little boy, suddenly curious.

"Nothing, honey," his mother reassured him. "Just a little short on butter."

·

What's a 79?
   Sixty-nine with ten-percent tax.

·

What's the definition of a cigar?
   Breath freshener for people who eat shit.

·

A number of tequilas at the Mexican restaurant had loosened the young woman's inhibitions, so as soon as she and her date had arrived back at her apartment, she proposed, "Let's do sixty-nine!"

"What's sixty-nine?" he asked, naive but willing.

"Just put your face right here," she instructed, spreading

118

her legs. Unfortunately, the refried beans had begun to take effect, and just as the young man obeyed her instructions, she farted. The fellow lifted up his head for a big breath but dutifully lowered it again, only to get another blast in the face. Nearly passing out, he took another deep breath, but after several more farts he changed his mind about the whole operation. "Hey, where're you going?" asked the woman, seeing him pulling on his pants.

"No offense, lady," he told her, "but I don't think I could take sixty-four more of those."

.

The precocious kid walked into a bar and yelled to the waitress to bring him a martini straight up, on the double.

"Cool it, kid," said the waitress, coming over. "Whaddaya wanna do, get me in trouble?"

"Maybe later," replied the eight-year-old, "but right now I'd like that drink."

.

What do you call an onion with whiplash?
   A tear jerker.

.

What's the difference between a casket and rubber?
   You come in one and go in the other.

"Now, children," admonished Miss Tuttle, the kindergarten teacher, "remember that you need to tell me if you need to go to the potty. Raise one finger if you have to tinkle and two if you have to poop, is that clear?"

She was irritated to see a small hand waving frantically from the rear of the classroom. "Yes, Billy, what's wrong?"

"Teacher, gimme a number, quick!" howled the kid. "I gotta fart!"

•

A New York motorist was stopped by a state trooper in deepest Georgia. "Gee, officer, I was only doing ten miles over the speed limit," he protested, walking over to the trooper's motorcycle. "Couldn't you just give me a warning?"

"Fine," drawled the trooper, and kicked him in the balls.

•

Ginny was less than pleased to get a postcard from her traveling salesman husband which read, "Sorry I'm not home yet, but I'm still buying."

"Well, you better get back home soon," she wrote back, "'cause I'm giving away what you're buying."

•

It started to rain heavily, so the construction worker came home early from the job, only to find his wife in bed with a professor from the community college. "Jesus, what the hell is going on here?" he screamed.

"See," said the wife, turning to her lover, "I *told* you he's an idiot."

TOO TASTELESS TO BE INCLUDED

Why are blacks so quick on their feet?

Because they spend their first nine months dodging coat hangers.

.

Frank and Phil were driving along a country road when their car broke down, so they got out and walked to the nearest farmhouse. The door was answered by an ugly middle-aged woman, who told them that she could provide a bed for one of them but that the other would have to sleep on the porch.

The two men had no option but to accept her offer, but as soon as she was out of earshot, Frank whispered, "I'm not sleeping with her."

"Me neither," Phil whispered back. So they agreed to flip for it, and Frank lost. And sure enough she grabbed for him as soon as he got into bed.

"Okay, lady, okay," he soothed, "but you gotta turn the lights off. I make love better in the dark." And as she went over to the switch, he spotted a bushel of corn on the cob in the corner of the room. As soon as the room was dark he grabbed an ear and began shoving it into her pussy, but pretty soon it started to get soggy. Terrified that she'd wise up and reach for the shotgun under the bed, he tossed the corncob out the window, grabbed another, and kept at it until he'd used up the last ear and she was sound asleep.

The next day they got the car repaired and were rolling down the highway when Frank burst out laughing at the thought of last night's exploits.

"What the hell's so funny?" asked his buddy. "While you were in getting laid, I was out on the porch eating buttered corn on the cob all night."

•

Know why there's no toilet paper at Colonel Sanders's restaurants?

'Cause it's finger-lickin' good!

•

If a truckload of dead babies is gross, and a live one at the bottom eating its way out is grosser than gross, what's grossest of all?

When he goes back for seconds.

Little Jack Horner sat in the corner
Rubbing his grandma's twat
   Stuck in his pinky
   Got it all sticky
And said, "Damn—you're beginning to rot."

             ·

Bill left a used rubber on the dashboard of his car, and as he was picking up speed, it blew out the window. Looking out the rearview mirror, he saw a little kid pick it up, so he backed up to where the kid was standing. "Listen, kid, I'll give you a buck for your Twinkie," he offered. The kid turned his back on the car, thought it over, and turned back to Bill.

   "Okay, mister," he agreed. Running home, the kid found his mother in the kitchen. "Hey, Ma, guess what?" he shouted. "Some guy gave me a dollar for a Twinkie he dropped—and I licked out all the cream filling before I gave it back!"

             ·

"What's the trouble, sonny?" asked the kindly old gent of the little boy crying his heart out on the curb.

   "A drunk puked over there," sobbed the boy, "and my brother Phil's getting all the big pieces."

   "Never mind," said the old man consolingly, pulling out

his wallet. "Here's a dollar. Go buy a loaf of bread and you can sop up the juice."

.

What's grosser than gross?
  Two vampires fighting over a used tampax.

.

What's *really* grosser than gross?
  When you stick a baby in boiling water feet first and watch his brains blow through his soft spot.

.

"Mommy, Mommy, why are you moaning?"
  "Shut up and keep licking!"

The series that redefines the meaning of the word *"gross"*!

Blanche Knott's

Truly Tasteless Jokes

Over 4 million copies of
***Truly Tasteless Jokes* in print!**

TRULY TASTELESS JOKES IV
_____ 90365-0 $2.95 U.S.   _____ 90366-9 $3.50 Can.

TRULY TASTELESS JOKES V
_____ 90371-5 $2.95 U.S.   _____ 90372-3 $3.50 Can.

TRULY TASTELESS JOKES VI
_____ 90361-8 $2.95 U.S.   _____ 90373-1 $3.75 Can.

TRULY TASTELESS JOKES VII
_____ 90765-6 $2.95 U.S.   _____ 90766-4 $3.95 Can.

TRULY TASTELESS JOKES VIII
_____ 91058-4 $2.95 U.S.   _____ 91059-2 $3.95 Can.

Publishers Book and Audio Mailing Service
P.O. Box 120159, Staten Island, NY 10312-0004

Please send me the book(s) I have checked above. I am enclosing
$ _____ (please add $1.25 for the first book, and $.25 for each
additional book to cover postage and handling. Send check or
money order only—no CODs.)

Name _____

Address _____

City _____ State/Zip _____

Please allow six weeks for delivery. Prices subject to change
without notice.   TTJ 1/89

READ
MY
LIPS.

The Wit & Wisdom of
GEORGE
BUSH

With some reflections by Dan Quayle

edited by Ken Brady & Jeremy Solomon